BRITISH AIRFIELDS OF THE SECOND WORLD WAR

Stuart Hadaway

SHIRE PUBLICATIONS

Bloomsbury Publishing Plc

PO Box 883, Oxford, OX1 9PL, UK

1385 Broadway, 5th Floor, New York, NY 10018, USA

E-mail: shire@bloomsbury.com

www.shirebooks.co.uk

SHIRE is a trademark of Osprey Publishing Ltd

First published in Great Britain in 2020

A catalogue record for this book is available from the British Library.

ISBN: PB 978 1 78442 395 7

      eBook 978 1 78442 396 4

      ePDF 978 1 78442 393 3

      XML 978 1 78442 394 0

20 21 22 23 24   10 9 8 7 6 5 4 3 2 1

Typeset by PDQ Digital Media Solutions, Bungay, UK

Printed and bound in India by Replika Press Private Ltd.

COVER IMAGE
Front cover: Supermarine Spitfire Vb AB910 at RAF Coltishall in Norfolk, 1967. It was used in the film *Battle of Britain*, a 1969 production recreating the Second World War air campaign (Photo by Keith Hamshere/Getty Images). Back cover: Reproduction airfield orientation plan (Lincolnshire Aviation Heritage Centre).

TITLE PAGE IMAGE
An officer watches from the window of a control tower as a crew walks onto an airfield past the 'landing T' and signal square.

CONTENTS PAGE IMAGE
A Sergeant signaller watches as a Handley Page Halifax of No. 1663 Heavy Conversion Unit comes in to land at RAF Holme-in-Spalding, 1943. Such rudimentary radio/telephone kit was commonly used for flying control throughout the war.

ACKNOWLEDGEMENTS:
All images are courtesy of the Air Historical Branch (RAF), except for those appearing on the following pages, which are the author's own: 5, 6, 10, 17 (bottom), 27, 29, 32, 36, 49, 58 (all), 59 (both), 60, 61 (both), 62 and 63.

CONTENTS

INTRODUCTION: THE UNSINKABLE AIRCRAFT CARRIER

An Avro Lancaster from No. 550 Squadron takes off from RAF North Luffenham on a raid, 1944.

BY THE END OF 1945, over 600 military airfields were scattered across the UK. They constituted a vast outlay of money, resources, and personnel, but it had been worth every man, woman, penny, and brick. Those airfields had secured victory for Britain and the Allies.

The survival of Britain in 1940 was perhaps the most crucial turning point of the Second World War. It may not have seemed like it at the time, and Pearl Harbour, the Battle of Midway, Stalingrad, El Alamein, Kursk, and the Normandy

landings were all still needed to ultimately secure victory, but without the survival of Britain they would arguably have never happened. If the Germans could have focused their entire attention on attacking the Soviets in 1941 (and Britain had not been there to send vital supplies to help them), Russia might well have fallen. Adolf Hitler would have been undisputed ruler of Europe. Even after the US had defeated Japan, it is unlikely they would have been able to launch the liberation of Europe across the breadth of the Atlantic. Britain ensured victory by its very survival let alone its more pro-active efforts to defeat the enemy.

One of the sets of Coupled General Service Sheds (hangars) at IWM Duxford.

An important part of this role was as a base for aircraft. From Britain, maritime patrol aircraft kept the Atlantic open, allowing supplies and troops to pour into the UK. Both Royal Air Force (RAF) and United States Army Air Force (USAAF) bombers pounded Germany, destroying

Many former
airfields are
marked by
memorials.
This one is for
RAF Mepal in
Cambridgeshire.

industry and diverting massive amounts of resources from
the fighting fronts to the defence of German skies. Then, in
1944–45, air armadas launched from the UK led the way in
the fight to liberate France and then Holland, and finally to
invade Germany itself. These vast numbers of aircraft needed
hundreds of airfields – known officially as 'stations' – of
myriad shapes and sizes from which to operate, and a great
infrastructure to support them.

Today, the remains of those airfields are amongst the
most visible reminders of the war in many areas of the
UK. The shadows of runways can be seen in fields, and
surviving buildings of many different original types are still
in use as farm buildings, warehouses, or even coffee shops.
Many former airfields are marked by memorials, and a few
have been turned into museums dedicated to the British,
Commonwealth, and American personnel who lived on
them, flew from them, and if they were lucky, returned
safely to them. This book provides an introduction to those
airfields, how they operated, and what it was like to live
and work on them.

FROM WOOD TO STONE

BASIC GRASS MILITARY airfields sprang up across the UK
from late 1914, as the Royal Flying Corps (RFC) and
Royal Naval Air Service (RNAS) sought to rapidly expand
their tiny forces. Some of the new air stations were based on
civilian sites, such as Hendon, where flying schools and aircraft
workshops already existed. Most were formed by buying
farmland, draining and flattening it, and erecting wooden
sheds and canvas tents to serve as offices, workshops, hangars,
and living accommodation. Sometimes farm buildings could
be utilised, but facilities were mostly built from scratch. When
the RAF was formed by amalgamating the RFC and RNAS

RAF Bircham
Newton in 1927,
showing the
standard airfield
layout of landing
ground and
hangars, with the
Technical Site
behind them and
the Domestic
Site slightly
detached.

on 1 April 1918, it took over these airfields. After the end of the war most were disposed of and returned to farmland or civilian use.

Some remained in military hands, and began to be developed. The Chief of the Air Staff from 1919 to 1930, Sir Hugh Trenchard, poured a massive amount of his meagre resources into the solid foundations of these bases. Wooden shacks were replaced, sometimes by grandiose mock-Georgian stone structures, the designs for which were submitted for approval to the Royal Fine Arts Commission. Although criticised in the austere 1920s as a waste of money, logic and sense had been applied: stone was used for barrack blocks, Officers' Messes, Station Headquarters, and other permanent buildings where the solid walls improved comfort and reduced maintenance costs. Many of these structures are still in use on RAF stations today, while blocks built in more recent decades crumble around them. Workshops and hangars, meanwhile, which might need to be adapted or enlarged for new aircraft types or equipment, usually remained constructed of either wood or metal sheets.

Not only did Trenchard's airfields instil a sense of permanence and longevity to his fledgling service, but they

The Married Quarters at RAF Henlow, 1930s.

also provided a solid basis from which to operate. The new, permanent airfields were an investment in the future, giving his force the accommodation it needed to start slowly building a world-class force.

Airfields followed a set pattern, albeit one that was adjustable to local terrain and conditions. The airfield itself was a simple flat field – an open stretch of well-drained grassland as long as it was wide, on which aircraft could take off or land in any direction, depending on the wind. The direction of the wind was indicated by a 'landing T'. These were T-shaped panels laid on the ground near the station Watch Office (with the cross bar facing into the wind) along with a 'signal square' – a clearly marked area containing any other pertinent signals. Both could easily be seen from the air. The Watch Office was simply a hut where the duty officer would be, booking aircrew and aircraft in or out on take-off or landing, and keeping track of flight plans, the weather, and other relevant details. In the absence of ground-to-air radios, flying control (i.e. giving instructions to aircraft in the air over the airfield) was limited to these panels, or perhaps firing flares to warn of imminent danger to a landing aircraft. Next to the Watch Office would be a shed for fire engines and other emergency vehicles, ready to respond to crashes or other incidents on the airfield. The only general rule while in the air was that aircraft were to fly around the airfield in an anti-clockwise pattern, but even this was subject to local variations.

Along the edge of the airfield ran the hangars. On a bomber station, there would usually be four large hangars. A typical bomber station had two squadrons of two 'flights' each, and each flight would have its own hangar where routine maintenance was carried out and aircraft were stored at night. Fighter stations usually had fewer, slightly smaller hangars, reflecting the smaller size of their aircraft. Small workshops were built into the hangars along the walls, allowing a certain amount of work to be done next to the aircraft.

For deeper maintenance, or work on non-aircraft equipment, there would be a Technical Site just behind the hangars, including workshops, storerooms, and other specialist buildings. Each station had to be as close to self-sufficient as possible, with its own small power station or generator, and water tower.

Behind the Technical Site was the Domestic Site: barrack blocks for the airmen and Non-Commissioned Officers (NCOs), the Officers' Mess where unmarried officers 'lived in', and married quarters for all ranks. The airmen and corporals had a Mess Hall for eating, above which was a library and a games room, while senior NCOs and officers ate in their own messes. The Station Headquarters generally stood near the Main Gate, and near it a naval-type mast was used to fly the RAF Ensign during daylight hours. 'Main Gate' was a figurative term for the main entrance, and few stations during the inter-war period had actual gates. Next to this entrance was the Main Guard Room, which monitored traffic in and out of the station and was manned around the clock, as was the fire section just behind it.

The 1932 Main Guard Room at IWM Duxford.

A Boulton Paul Overstrand in the mid-1930s, with a 'C'-type hangar under construction behind.

Flying boat bases were different, in that the 'runway' was a stretch of water. Ramps ran into sheltered water, with the hangars on the shore, and then a standard range of technical and domestic buildings behind. The small number of airship stations were similar to normal airfields, but had tall masts for mooring the airships, and greatly enlarged hangars.

In 1934 it became clear that there was a growing threat from Germany, and the RAF and Air Ministry instigated a series of Expansion Plans. New airfields sprang up around the country during what became known as the Expansion Period. Officers charged with opening new stations would report to the Air Ministry to receive reams of standardised building plans, tailored to the type and function of the airfield in question. While local modifications were allowed – and indeed were common – standardisation helped keep costs down, and also added a large degree of uniformity across stations. This allowed personnel to find familiar working environments as they arrived at their new stations, aiding operational efficiency.

A Fairey Battle in front of an inter-war 'C'-type hangar. Later hangars dispensed with the large windows and the gabled roof, both of which were dangerous during air raids.

AIRFIELD 1940

A T THE OUTBREAK of war, the vast majority of the RAF's 158 UK airfields were still grass fields. Concrete areas could be found around the hangars on most airfields, and rough tracks for taxiways around the edges, but few had all-weather hardened runways. In the 1920s and 1930s the grass had allowed under-powered and primitive aircraft to take off at the most advantageous angle to make full use of the wind. In 1940, these grass runways were rapidly becoming out-dated as heavier, more powerful aircraft needed a firmer surface and were better able to cope in less-than-ideal wind conditions. The RAF began a massive programme to pave their airfields, although in the short term grass was still useful for fighter and training units at least. During the Battle of Britain, fighters caught by surprise on the ground could scatter and take off in great numbers with little chance of collisions, and no matter how many bombs were dropped on the grass it was practically impossible for the Germans to completely close the airfield. There would almost always be, somewhere, a long enough stretch on un-cratered grass for aircraft to land.

Paving was started in earnest, though, and was a massive investment. Not only were runways built (each bomber airfield receiving three runways in a triangle, each 914 metres [1,000 yards] long and 46 metres [50 yards] wide), but also perimeter tracks, taxiways, and dispersal sites. 'Landing Ts' were now to be placed at the end of the runway to be used, to show the landing and wind directions. At the start of hostilities,

Vickers
Wellingtons
of No. 149
Squadron, RAF
Mildenhall, at the
start of the war.
Even the RAF's
heaviest bombers
operated mainly
from grass
airfields.

aircraft were moved out of their peace-time lodgings in the
hangars, and kept dispersed around the airfield wherever
possible, to limit the damage a single German bomb could
do. However, this required the building of hardstanding for
them to sit on, shelters and basic facilities for the ground crew,
and for the crews awaiting word to 'scramble' into the air.
On some fighter stations, 'E'-type pens sprang up. These were

Hawker
Hurricanes of
No. 1 Squadron
in an 'E'-type pen
at RAF Wittering,
1940.

A 'dispersal' at RAF Wick, 1940, with pilots of No. 111 Squadron waiting by their Hawker Hurricanes.

twin bays formed by brick walls covered in thick mounds of earth, with an air-raid shelter built into the rear wall. Two fighters could be housed in each pen.

Dispersing aircraft was not the only wartime change on airfields. Other elements were dispersed where possible, with fuel, bomb, and ammunition stores being moved further from the main sites and each other. The new airfields that were springing up across the country were much more spread out in their basic design, with the hangars (which were prime targets) further apart, and the technical and domestic sites being widely separated.

Defensive structures also sprang up, or in many cases down. Air raid shelters were dug into the ground, and covered in thick layers of earth. Slit-trenches were dug near dispersals, hangars, and other buildings, to give the occupants somewhere to take shelter during raids. Warning would be given by wailing sirens, re-purposed from the fire warning system. Airfield perimeters, which pre-war had usually simply consisted of hedges, were now reinforced by barbed wire fences, and Main Gates acquired actual gates and checkpoints. Pillboxes were sited to cover the airfield itself in case of enemy airborne landings, as well as the approaches to the station. Most were built to standard designs, although the rush to build airfield defences as Britain suddenly fell under threat of invasion led to local, improvised patterns also being used. Some very complicated types were built, including the Pickett Hamilton Fort, a round pillbox that could be lowered into the ground when not in use. When wanted, it was raised by a pneumatic jack.

Defences were manned by personnel from the station, given hasty small arms training, as well as soldiers drawn from Home Guard or regular units. Soldiers also manned anti-aircraft guns, both inside and outside the airfield perimeter, usually dug in to sandbagged emplacements. At some airfields, Parachute and Cable (PAC) Rocket batteries were used. PACs trailed thick cables as they shot into the air, which then descended slowly on parachutes, designed to damage wings and foul the propellers of attacking aircraft. The defences were controlled, or perhaps more accurately co-ordinated, from a Battle Headquarters; this was an underground bunker built at a location where a turret gave a good view of the airfield, and connected to the defences by telephone.

Apart from making airfields more defensible, efforts were made to make them harder for enemy bombers to find. Black

Taking stock in a bomb store. The coming of war soon proved existing facilities woefully inadequate, and bomb stores were rapidly expanded.

Test-firing the guns of a Supermarine Spitfire in the 'butts' at RAF Digby, 1940.

and green camouflage paint was applied to airfield buildings to break up their outlines and allow them to blend into the surrounding countryside; the remains of this paint can still be seen on buildings at the RAF Museum at Hendon. Runways, where they existed, were also painted to look like fields. At RAF Northolt, on the western edge of London, the station commander felt that the rural camouflage would just make his airfield stand out more among the suburbs. Instead, he painted houses on the fronts and sides of his hangars, and street layouts

The old parachute packing shed at the RAF Museum, Hendon. Many of the wartime buildings at Hendon retain the vestiges of their camouflage.

Vickers Wellingtons of No. 149 Squadron fly over 'C'-type hangars draped in camouflage netting.

on their roofs. A stream was painted meandering down the two concrete runways (which had been laid that summer) and a pond was later painted on their intersection. According to the station commander's memoir (*Flying Fever* by Air Vice Marshal Stanley Vincent, the only British pilot to claim combat victories in both world wars), the camouflage was so effective that one day two swans 'crash landed' while trying to alight on the pond.

Even with these passive and active defences, airfields remained terribly vulnerable to air attack, especially in southern and eastern England. During and after the Battle of Britain, the German Air Force specifically targeted airfields. Not everyone was able to take cover during raids, and many men and women stayed at their posts to keep the airfields operational. Although serving at Rye Radar Station rather than an airfield, the experiences of this anonymous member of the Women's Auxiliary Air Force (WAAF) on 13 August 1940 capture the terror of being under aerial attack:

The deep, snarling roar of the bombers and the protecting fighters grew closer and closer till the whole hut vibrated with it ... Suddenly the RAF Officer-in-Charge called: 'They're diving! Get down!' and only then did those airwomen move, and they moved as if you'd pressed a button! We all fell flat on the floor as the first stick of bombs burst ... Everything loose shot off the tables, shutters were blown in, and glass flew in every direction. The floor and hut shuddered, and chairs and tables overturned onto us. Through clouds of dust I saw legs and arms protruding from underneath the debris; to those in reach I gave a friendly pat and an assurance that they were all right and must remain still ... Just then another full-blasted roar which seemed to be coming right on to the hut, followed by a terrible and shattering explosion; doors and the remaining windows were swept away, and then huge lumps of things began crashing through the walls, high up where the sandbags didn't reach, and through the windowless spaces.

These three WAAFs each received Military Medals for remaining at their posts at RAF Biggin Hill while under heavy attack during the Battle of Britain. The damage caused by bombing can be seen on the building behind.

The dedication of their personnel meant that very few airfields were ever closed for more than a few hours due to enemy action. Even while under attack, they could remain operational. Sergeant Iain Hutchinson, a pilot with No. 54 Squadron at RAF Hornchurch, recalled landing his aircraft:

... the airfield was under attack and chunks of shrapnel were raining down on the airfield. When I taxied towards the dispersal no-one was to be seen; they were all in the air-raid shelters taking cover. Before I

The controlled explosion of a German bomb at RAF Hemswell, August 1940. Note the station water tower to the left.

rolled to a halt and cut the engine, 'B' Flight ground crew, under their Flight Sergeant, were swarming around my Spitfire; the bowser was racing out to refuel the aircraft, while the armament men, laden with ammunition, were reloading the guns. The noise from the explosions going on around us was terrifying, but not one of those magnificent men faltered for a moment in their tasks. I was frankly relieved to be taking off again.

Each aircraft had an assigned Fitter to look after the engine, and a Rigger to maintain the airframe, while armourers, refuellers, and other specialists would be assigned to a flight of several aircraft. They became intensely attached to 'their' aircraft, as an anonymous Flight Sergeant from No. 249 Squadron told the BBC in 1940:

Everybody is very proud of the fighter in his charge. And a healthy rivalry develops, too…. Once a pilot came back from a battle after shooting down a Junkers 88 and two Messerschmitts. The crew that serviced that Hurricane did a war dance and went about swanking to the other crews. They regarded the three at one crack as THEIR work.

We work long hours, but we don't mind. Our day starts at dawn…. The fitter gets into the cockpit and the rigger stands by the starting-motor. The engine is started up and run until warm. Then, should there be an alarm, there will be no trouble about starting the aircraft or getting it off the ground quickly.

Suppose there is an alarm. The message comes through by telephone and immediately I dash out and shout the signal for every crew to go to their own particular aircraft and start up. At the same time the pilots come from their crew-room and scramble into their aircraft. Sometimes the pilot arrives at the same time as the crew, but as often as not the engine is started when he races up. If it takes more than two and a half minutes from the warning to the time all the aircraft are in the air – well, there is usually an inquest at which I am the coroner …

As soon as the first one lands it taxis towards the waiting ground crew. A tanker goes alongside to fill up the petrol tanks. At the same time the armourers re-arm the eight Browning guns. The rigger changes the oxygen bottles and fits the starting-motor to the aircraft so that it is ready for the next take-off. Then the rigger takes some strips of fabric which he has brought with him from the crew-room and places them over the gun holes. It helps keep the guns clean and also helps to keep the aircraft 100 per cent efficient in the air until the guns are fired.

Meanwhile, another member of the crew searches the aircraft for bullet holes and the electrician goes over the wiring and the wireless mechanic tests the radio set. Every little part of the aircraft is OK before the machine is

Ground crews from No. 601 Squadron work on 'their' Hawker Hurricane, RAF Exeter, 1940. By then, all routine maintenance work was done in the open rather than in vulnerable hangars.

pronounced serviceable again. All this process should take no more than five minutes, but we allow seven minutes for the whole job….

Finally, at nightfall, we make the daily inspection. The armourers clean the guns, the fitter checks the engine over, the rigger checks round the fuselage and cleans it, and the wireless man checks the radio set. The instruments man checks the instruments. When everything is OK and the necessary papers signed, the machine can be put to bed. The sleeves are put on the wings, the cover is put over the cockpit, the pickets are pegged into the ground and the machine left, heading into the wind, until dawn…. During the summer-time our hours are from about three-thirty am until ten-thirty pm.

Behind those working on the aircraft were hundreds more men and women, some working before and after the ground crews. Cooks, firemen, parachute packers, cleaners, and clerks all kept the aircrews and ground crews supplied with what they needed to keep flying and fighting. Most stations buzzed with activity around the clock, especially those that operated bombers or night fighters.

Night flying had been rare in the inter-war period – it was dangerous work, after all. The outbreak of war led to a steep increase in night flying, needing stations to adapt to the new work. Lights – often initially cut-off tins full of burning petrol or 'goose-necked' paraffin lamps, but later electric lights controlled from a central panel – marked the runways, although these also highlighted the airfield as a target to enemy aircraft. Lights were added to mark the approaches to the airfield, and to warn of dangers. It had been rare pre-war for tall buildings to carry hazard lights, but now red lamps were placed on tall buildings near airfields. Often this meant the spire of the local village church, much to the hilarity of the villagers, for whom red lights had previously only had a very different, distinctly non-clerical meaning.

From 1940, only major work was undertaken in hangars – they were too vulnerable to enemy attack to risk packing with aircraft.

WARTIME GROWTH

THE BUILDING OF airfields between 1934, when the Expansion Period began, and 1945 was one of the largest single construction schemes the country has ever seen. Take East Anglia as an example. In 1934, there had been four front-line stations in the region. By 1939, there were fifteen front-line stations and five 'satellite' stations (essentially, overflow sites with limited facilities). By 1944, there were 107 front-line stations in East Anglia.

The bare facts of this wartime growth are staggering:

- Across the UK, the number of RAF airfields rose from 158 in 1939 to 490 in 1945, plus 133 USAAF airfields (all but 14 of which had been built by the Air Ministry), as well as a handful of airfields for the Royal Navy's Fleet Air Arm.
- Some 1.3 billion man-hours went into building these airfields.
- At the height of the building programme in 1942, it comprised just over one third of Britain's daily expenditure on the war.
- A single bomber airfield would take 130,000 tons of cement and ballast to build, as well as 50 miles of drainage pipes and cable conduits.
- By March 1945, 36,000 acres of concrete and tarmac paving and trackways had been laid on British airfields, enough at that time to completely cover

OPPOSITE
Civilian contractors working for the Air Ministry clear the site for RAF Heathrow.

Edinburgh (32,000 acres) and nearly cover Birmingham (39,000 acres).

- In 1942, 127,000 people – nearly one third of the UK's total building and civil engineering workforce – were engaged on construction for the Air Ministry.

Stations would be built by the Air Ministry Works Directorate, using a range of civilian contractors. Before any building work could start, a massive area needed to be cleared and prepared. The land needed to be flattened, soft areas made firm, and drainage systems installed. Only after a massive amount of preparatory work could actual building begin. Plans for stations and buildings were standardised, but there was considerable leeway to make modifications and changes appropriate to local conditions.

In early 1941 the RAF formed a series of 'Works Squadrons', each initially consisting of ten 80-man Works Flights. With very little machinery and a largely unskilled workforce, at first they were used for repairing bomb damage on stations. But the squadrons were gradually moved into airfield construction work. Recruiting trained and skilled tradesmen, in early 1942

The main drainage pipes being laid at RAF Heathrow, 1944.

Men of the Heavy Plant Depot of the RAF ACS, including Sergeant John Hadaway, standing on the left.

they began to receive heavy plant equipment. Soon, thirty squadrons were formed, grouped into Wings of three Airfield Construction Squadrons supported by a Plant Squadron. Each Wing totalled nearly 2,500 personnel. In 1943, the organisation officially became the RAF Airfield Construction Service (ACS), complete with a training school and heavy plant depot at RAF Mill Green (near Hatfield). Many ACS personnel were subsequently posted to build airfields overseas, and the bulk of airfield construction work in the UK continued to be done by civilian firms.

Not only did the number of stations rapidly increase, but the size of each station also grew. A bomber station went from having a permanent staff of 1,143 in 1940, to 2,500 in 1945. New accommodation and facilities were needed for the new staff, while separate sites had to be built to accommodate and cater for the growing numbers of women of the WAAF. Larger and more complicated aircraft led to a greater need for technical buildings and workshops, and bigger bomb, fuel, and ammunition storage facilities. More aircrew needed bigger briefing rooms, larger equipment stores, and more space for drying and packing parachutes. By the end of the war, the average station encompassed more than 500 buildings.

Office space became crowded as more staff were crammed into them (as here, in the Intelligence Section at RAF High Wycombe).

Wartime stations were also spread out over larger areas. Hangars and buildings in the Technical Site were built further apart, so that enemy bombs would do less damage. New-build Domestic Sites in particular were often built separately, away from the main airfield, and personnel would face a short commute to work.

More aircraft and bigger crews meant more aircrew equipment; parachute packing sheds became more like warehouses.

Not all new airfields were built to a full scale. Satellite airfields were built near to existing stations and under their administrative control as an easy way to expand capacity. Consisting of a runway and basic maintenance buildings, they were essentially an overflow from the main airfield. They needed half as many staff to operate, and were obviously much cheaper to build than a full airfield, although many were developed over time until they did become fully fledged independent stations.

Relief Landing Grounds were a similar idea, used early in the war by training units before large-scale aircrew training was moved overseas. These were even more basic, and simply provided extra runways for trainees to fly 'circuits and bumps', practising take-offs and landings. Satellite Landing Grounds, meanwhile, were used by Maintenance Units to hold aircraft waiting to be assigned to squadrons. These were kept as undeveloped as possible in order to make them almost invisible from the air, and so avoid the attention of the enemy. Advanced Landing Grounds were opened in large numbers in southern England in 1943 and 1944 to provide temporary

Nissen huts were endlessly versatile and could be modified to many uses. This surviving one at IWM Duxford housed a Link Trainer flight simulator.

Life on an Advanced Landing Ground was very basic – essentially, field conditions.

bases for the huge numbers of aircraft that would be needed for the liberation of France. These usually had a temporary runway of metal matting and tented accommodation and facilities. Apart from keeping them cheap and easy to build, this was also valuable experience for when basic airfields would need to be built and operated close behind the front lines in Europe.

Three Emergency Landing Grounds were also designated, at RAF Manston in Kent, RAF Carnaby in Yorkshire, and RAF Woodbridge in Suffolk. These were purpose-built for damaged aircraft returning from sorties over occupied Europe and Germany to divert to, and so prevent damaged aircraft from blocking runways at their home stations while the rest of their squadron was trying to land. They had specially widened and lengthened runways, and very little in the way of ground staff, buildings or equipment beyond the fire, medical, and heavy lift capability that their role required.

One of the more common buildings still found on old airfields is the control tower – although this term did not come into general usage until late in the war. Known originally as Watch Offices, these were usually wooden huts where

Pigeon baskets being prepared for issue; should a crew be shot down over the sea, the homing pigeon could carry a message with their position back to the UK.

arriving aircrew reported in, and departing ones checked out. As such, they were near the edge of the landing ground and contained briefing rooms, meteorological offices, and other administrative sections. From the start of the Expansion Period in 1934, these buildings became more substantial, multi-floor brick structures, sometimes with viewing platforms or verandas. They came in seven standard patterns, but many had

Pilots of No. 19 Squadron at RAF Fowlmere rest outside Nissen huts in 1940.

The 1941-pattern Couple Type T2 Aircraft Sheds (hangars) at IWM Duxford. These wartime hangars were much quicker and cheaper to build than the older brick-built ones.

local modifications or were simply built to their own design. However, with their blocky structure and large windows, they are distinctive whatever their design.

From around 1935, RAF aircraft started to become fitted with air-to-ground radios as standard, and so the station staff could begin to exercise some genuine control over their own air space. Radio rooms were placed in the control towers, and the duty officers would give permissions for take-offs and landings, including organising the holding patterns overhead, transmitting using a two-letter code or a codename to identify their airfield. Controllers only had jurisdiction over the immediate area of their airfield, beyond which Sector and Group Operations Rooms took over responsibility.

Hangars are another common building type still to be found on old airfields, and they also remain highly identifiable despite coming in myriad different styles and sizes. As the Second World War approached, the sturdy brick-built hangars were replaced by metal-framed hangars that were skinned in corrugated metal sheets, which were quicker and cheaper to build. Sloping roofs were introduced to help deflect falling bombs. Many of the standard hangar types came in a variety of sub-types, with the size and height of the hangar and the doors being adjusted to the types of aircraft that needed to be housed. The metal walls meant that discrete workshops were no longer built into the edges, and work benches and tools would be kept in the hangar itself for basic repair work. An even more basic type of hangar, the 'Blister' hangar, also came into use. This had a simple roof that sloped right down to the ground, and just canvas curtains (if anything) at either end. These too came in a variety of sizes.

Wherever possible, aircraft were taken into the hangars only for significant repair or major maintenance (and even then, for any really extensive work the aircraft would be taken away from the airfield). Routine maintenance and minor repairs were done in the open air or under basic shelters at the dispersals. This could be difficult and unpleasant, working in all weathers and year round on what were, by definition, windy and exposed areas. For maritime units it was even worse. Such work could be conducted on flying boats while they were moored, with not only the elements but also the movement of the water to deal with. Maintenance staff would tie their tools to their belts or to the aircraft with ropes to avoid losing them into the water from numbed fingers or a sudden wave.

Personnel working on a Short Sunderland – difficult enough in calm weather, but positively dangerous in rough seas.

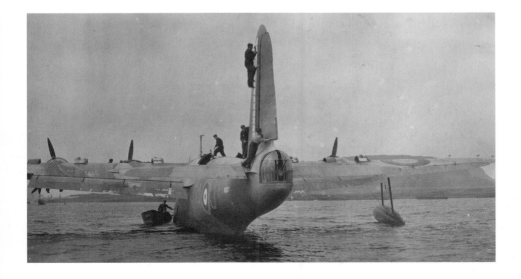

AIRFIELD LIFE

AIRFIELD LIFE WAS dictated by many factors: the role of the airfield for example affected shift patterns and the size of the staff. It must also be remembered that stations were military units, and as such discipline and military formalities had to be taken into account. Organisationally, the station could be complicated. The Station Commander, usually a Group Captain in rank, was responsible for the fabric, infrastructure, and personnel of the station itself, aided by the Station Warrant Officer (or 'SWO'), the senior NCO on site. However, squadrons on the airfield had their own command structures, and reported to their own superiors on operational matters. Bomber stations commonly had two squadrons, each commanded by a Wing Commander who reported to their own separate Group command structure. In Fighter Command, the squadrons on a station often formed their own Wing, and the commander of that Wing again reported up to his Group structure. This could make matters of administrative command and discipline tricky, as there were parallel command structures and not everyone would be obliged to follow the orders of someone in a different reporting chain. As a rule, though, you crossed the SWO at your peril, regardless of your rank or position.

Accommodation at RAF airfields came in a variety of types, most of which were basic. The luckier personnel slept in pre-war brick-built barrack blocks. During the Expansion Period, barracks were usually built as two-storey units (although some

OPPOSITE
WAAF Quarters
in a barrack
block at RAF
Henlow.

Nissen huts were one of many different types of small temporary structures thrown up in great numbers during the war.

had three storeys). The length of the blocks varied, but they were divided into rooms for 25–30 airmen each, plus small rooms for attendant NCOs, and possibly a communal room. Standard blocks held eight NCOs and either 56 or 84 men. In many cases, parallel blocks were joined by a two-storey ablutions block containing toilets, washrooms, and laundry rooms to form an 'H' block. Officers and senior NCOs had their own blocks or slept in their relevant messes, and generally had private or semi-private rooms. Married personnel of all ranks had allotted houses, albeit sized to fit their rank, or could arrange to 'live out' in a local town or village.

Wartime brought a distinct downturn in the standards of accommodation. The speed of expansion led to huts being thrown up to house extra personnel, in a myriad of similar wooden or sheet metal designs. The Nissen hut is probably the most famous of these. Built around basic frames and often curved in shape, they came in a range of sizes. With a concrete floor and a single stove in the centre for heating, they were thin walled, draughty, and retained little heat. Without running water or toilets, ablutions would be in a separate block relatively nearby. In 1939, accommodation was

Basic living conditions inside an accommodation hut at RAF Fowlmere, in 1940.

designed to allow officers 11 square metres (120 square feet), sergeants 6.5 square metres (70 square feet) and corporals or airmen 4.2 square metres (45 square feet) of personal space. This was reduced several times until finally in July 1943 it was fixed at 8.36 square metres (90 square feet) for officers and just 3 square metres (32 square feet) for corporals and airmen.

Inside the crew room of No. 605 Squadron at RAF Ford, where crews could relax while on and off duty.

In that space, each man had a bed, with a mattress that was formed of three square 'biscuits' laid along the frame. Above the bed was a shelf, under which would be hooks, and at the end of the bed might be a foot locker. Officers might be lucky enough to have a chair and desk. Aircrew would keep most of their flying kit in lockers in a crew room, where they would don it before an operation.

Life in a barrack block lacked privacy and comfort, although it was still better than being relegated to a hut. For personnel being posted from a pre-war station to a newly built one, it could come as shock, as Sergeant 'Goldie' Goldstraw, an Observer with No. 207 Squadron, found when his unit moved from RAF Waddington to RAF Bottesford:

> When we arrived the workmen were still finishing off many of the construction tasks, and there was liquid mud all over the place. Sleeping accommodation was very poor; the wooden huts were cold and draughty and let the rain in. The room which I shared with the rear gunner was often awash.... Bedding, clothing and personal effects were always damp, so we slept in trousers and shirts under the blankets.

A WAAF 'spud bashing'. Cookhouses would operate, at different levels of activity, around the clock.

Most of the time was spent in the Sergeants' Mess on the communal site where at least we could be warm and dry.

Working routines varied, with at least some personnel being active at any given time. Mechanics might need to be up early to prepare aircraft or other equipment for the day's duties, but cooks and other domestic staff had to be up even earlier. Likewise, staff could work far into the night, or even right around until dawn if waiting for bombers to return from operations. Some workers, like motor transport ('MT') drivers, could find themselves on duty for 48 hours, but spending most of that on 'standby' waiting to be called if needed.

Meals and breaks could be taken in a variety of ways. All stations had three messes, sorted by rank as the Officers', Sergeants' and Warrant Officers', and the Other Ranks' Messes, serving meals at set times. As members of the WAAF moved into active roles at airfields, a further three messes were created to cater to them, although this took time and initially many WAAFs used the same messes as the men (albeit carefully supervised to avoid inappropriate fraternisation). From 1942, this measure was abandoned to save on building costs and

The Orderly Office at RAF Duxford; such administrative staff were vital to keeping stations running, and kept regular, if long, office hours.

Inside an Airmen's Mess. This one, at RAF Halton, was in a considerably nicer building than most.

materials, and all messes and other communal areas became unisex. In 1943, messes were halved in size as a further savings measure, necessitating two sittings for each meal.

Food was fairly basic but carefully rationed and balanced. Additional food and hot drinks could be obtained through

A crew from No. 57 Squadron at RAF Scampton having bacon and eggs for breakfast in the early hours, having just returned from an operation over Germany, 1943.

the Navy, Army and Air Force Institute (NAAFI) canteen, as could other small items such as toiletries. Most stations had such a canteen, and some also had vans that would park by the hangars, dispersals, or other work areas to sell 'char and a wad' (a cup of tea and a sandwich) to workers taking quick breaks. Leading Aircraftwoman Daphne Forbes, an MT Driver at RAF Bottesford, recalled:

> Our own daily routine was more or less as follows. We got up at 6am, dressed, plodded over to the ablutions hut to wash, then returned to stack blankets, biscuits and sheets. We then tidied our bed space before getting out for working parade. We were not allowed to make our own beds until 4.30pm. Each hut housed about 30 bods with an NCO in a small room by the entrance…. We had no WAAF cookhouse or NAAFI on-site at first, so we had to walk or bike to the men's mess. Most of us missed breakfast and waited for the NAAFI wagon for 'char and a wad'.

While some work on the airfield could be mundane, working in such an environment was inherently dangerous. Enemy attack was always a possibility, particularly earlier in the war and in southern England. Friendly aircraft also posed

A NAAFI van dispensing tea and food at a dispersal, RAF Westhampnett, 1944.

Airfield work held all sorts of dangers, including severe weather. Here, ground crews prepare No. 257 Squadron Hawker Hurricanes in the snow at RAF Coltishall in January 1941.

a danger; crashes and other accidents happened, and could involve an aircraft hitting a building, vehicle, or pedestrian. Walking into a moving propeller was a not uncommon and usually fatal mistake. The blackout, imposed every night to stop lights from attracting enemy aircraft, was a constant hazard and source of casualties, from road or other accidents. Although kerbs, the edges of buildings and even trees were marked in white paint, collisions were almost inevitable.

Some areas obviously presented higher risks than others. Any work involving machinery had the potential to go wrong, while some work areas had far more volatile threats: bombs, fuel, and ammunition. Explosive and fuel dumps were kept well away from other buildings, and were surrounded by thick earth walls not only to protect them from outside interference, but also deflect any blasts within the compounds. Moving any of these materials was dangerous. Bombs were kept unfused, but these fuses (and tail units) were added before they left the dump and were towed on trolleys to waiting aircraft. Simple accidents or more complicated factors such as electrical or structural faults in the aircraft could see bombs being dropped while being loaded into an aircraft, and a fire starting during refuelling. It was relatively rare for a bomb to actually go off (although it did happen) but even so several hundred

Dangerous work: loading boxes of incendiary bombs onto a trailer.

kilograms of dead weight falling on an Armourer as he stood underneath it guiding it into the bomb bay could prove fatal. Sergeant W.D. Morgan recalled:

> The fusing was a dangerous job, for the bomb dump at Snaith, near Doncaster, had blown up twice in the same year ... and over 40 Armourers had been killed ... Normally, if a tail pistol cross threaded as you were putting it in you took it out again, but with the No. 39 anti-handling fuse a quarter of a turn backwards, or anti-clockwise, meant that you blew yourself up. So it was decided that only Senior NCOs would fuse these bombs in future, and when I did I cleared everyone else away, for even talking about the 'flicks' would distract one, as only one part turn to the left meant self-destruction. It's no wonder my hair's white ... Armourers had such dangerous jobs and so many died through bomb explosions that at one time we had to wear red bands on our arms, and when we approached aircraft to bomb up, other ground crew trades cleared off.

To counter the long hours, hard work, and dangers, a range of recreational facilities was provided on stations, or available off them. Libraries, squash courts, playing fields, and canteens were available on site for off-duty hours, although time off became increasingly rare. Pre-war, standard working days ran from 8am to 4.30pm, with Wednesday afternoons off for sports. Saturdays were generally quiet, and Sundays wherever possible kept as days of rest. This often remained the case for some months after the outbreak of war, but soon the standard working pattern had become 12-hour shifts (or longer, if the work needed doing) and six-and-a-half-day weeks. Time off was scarce and precious.

On isolated stations, extra facilities such as cinemas would be built, and concerts or dances would also be staged occasionally. Those lucky enough to be near a village or town would be able to obtain passes to leave the station on their afternoon off. Evenings out could also be arranged, signing out at the guard room after being inspected and passed as fit to be seen in public, and signing in again by 11.59pm. Most stations had one or more convenient gaps in the fences where airmen could make less official arrivals and departures. The one at RAF Linton-on-Ouse was next to a canal, and rumour has it that scores of RAF bicycles (issued to aid swift movement around the expanse of the airfields) still rest on the

Crashes were a constant danger. Here, fire crews struggle to free the pilot of a de Havilland Mosquito from No. 157 Squadron at RAF Predannack, 1944. An RAF chaplain is also in attendance.

Two pilots using the ubiquitous Air Ministry-issue bicycles to get around.

bed of the canal where airmen returning late ditched them rather than try to wrestle them through the hole in the fence. Weekend passes could also be obtained from time to time, perhaps allowing a fleeting visit home, or to the nearest city. Actual leave was granted at the rate of 61 days per year for aircrew, and 28 days per year for ground staff. These days would be issued in blocks of seven or 14 days, and were to be evenly distributed throughout the year.

AIRFIELD 1945

B Y 1945, THE average RAF airfield had grown not only in size, but also in complexity, technology, and capability. In simple terms, we have already seen how the number of buildings and personnel grew during the war. Landing areas, for example, went from mostly being open grass areas around 1,000 metres (3,300 feet) in diameter, to hard runways supported by taxiways and perimeter tracks. A standard 'Class A' bomber airfield now had three concrete runways, one 1,829 metres (2,000 yards) long and the other two 1,280 metres (1,400 yards) long, and all 46 metres (50 yards) wide. Even larger runways existed, and more were planned for Very Heavy Bomber use, or for long-range transport aircraft (including at RAF Heathrow).

But the mere concrete was only the tip of the runway iceberg. A few years before, aircraft had been left almost entirely to their own devices to land – guided by a 'landing T' and perhaps some lights. Now, an astonishing array of support was available. With ever more congested skies, and with airfields being built so close together in areas such as East Anglia and Lincolnshire, effective air traffic control became imperative.

Take-offs remained fairly low-tech if somewhat more intense than before. In 1940, a bomber station might have put up six or eight aircraft in a night, spread out over several hours. In 1945, two squadrons of up to 20 or even 30 aircraft each would take off at minute intervals. Then, as in 1940, permission would be asked for and given by flashing Aldis

OPPOSITE
Carefully lifting a 4,000lb bomb onto a trolley in just one bay of what would be an enormous bomb dump.

A Class 'A' airfield layout, with three runways plus taxiways and dispersals, in this case at RAF Marham, 1944.

lamps or firing coloured flares. Radio transmissions, which could be picked up by the enemy and warn of an impending raid, were still avoided. Signals might come straight from the control tower, or they could come from a controller in an airfield caravan. From mid-1942, it became increasingly common to site these caravans at the end of the active runway, partly to visibly mark which runway was in use, and partly to control traffic.

A crowded control tower, showing the numbers of staff and amount of technology needed to control a station's air space in 1945.

Landings, however, had become increasingly high-tech, especially at night or in bad weather. Aircraft could now be guided home over long distances. Lost aircraft could request a position 'fix' using a system called 'Darkie'. A call on a certain frequency would be plotted by the station, and they would confer with other airfields or Observer Corps sites to triangulate the signal, giving the pilot an accurate position from which they could navigate home. Closer to the airfield, radio was again used in the form of the 'Blind Approach Beam System' (BABS). Based on the pre-war Lorenz navigation system, this relied on a series of highly directional radio signals being 'beamed' out from the end of the runway. Receivers on the aircraft picked up the central beam, which triggered a continuous tone. If the aircraft drifted either left or right of the flight path, new beams which triggered either dots or dashes were picked up, allowing the pilot to track their drift and adjust course. Later, cross beams were added at set distances from the runway, so that the pilot could also check that their rate of descent was correct.

Elaborate systems of lights would also guide aircraft. Under the 'Sandra' system, three searchlights would be shone in a

The 1941-pattern control tower at IWM Duxford, which is still in daily use.

pyramid over an airfield, marking its location. Even in heavy cloud, the glow of the lights could usually be discerned from a considerable distance and used to home in on. 'Pundit' lights would flash the airfield's code-letters in Morse Code, allowing airfields to be positively identified. From 1941, Airfield Lighting Mk 1 (also commonly known as 'Drem Mk 1' lights, as they had been developed at RAF Drem) began to be installed. These consisted of an outer ring of lights around the airfield, from which a funnel of lights would guide the aircraft to the runway, which was itself lit. Unlike earlier systems, these lights were electric, and could be switched off in a heartbeat if it was discovered that enemy raiders were in the area. Later, a Mk 2 lighting system was developed, with the outer ring set at 6,035 metres (6,600 yards) from the airfield, and then a series of three funnels guiding the aircraft ever closer to the runway. At flying boat stations, equivalent sets of lights were secured on rafts or buoys. 'Chance' lights, essentially portable floodlights, could be used to give additional illumination on runways, and once on the perimeter track, dim, hooded lights (blue on the inner side, amber along the outer) guided aircraft back to dispersals.

Pilots of No. 2 Squadron consult the latest instructions, chalked on the side of an airfield caravan at RAF Cranfield.

Perhaps the most spectacular new airfield landing system was FIDO (Fog Investigation and Dispersal Operation). This consisted of perforated pipelines along the edges of a runway, through which petrol was pumped and then ignited. The resulting flames burned off fog to an altitude of several hundred feet, while the flames could be seen at a considerable distance. This allowed aircraft to find an airfield and land even in thick fog. It was ruinously expensive, burning 450,000 litres (100,000 gallons) of petrol per hour, and so FIDO was only installed at fifteen airfields in the UK, but from late 1943 it saved hundreds of aircraft and over 10,000 lives.

The new technologies allowed the airfields to operate around the clock, and in a far safer fashion. True air traffic control now became a realistic proposition. Control towers came into their own, guiding aircraft from many miles out, and having absolute control over all aircraft within 3,750 metres (3,000 yards) of the outer perimeter and up to 610 metres (2,000 feet) above the field.

While take-offs and landings perhaps best illustrate just how complex and technologically advanced airfields had become during the course of the war – moving from grass strips to something identifiable as a modern airfield in a mere five years – it remained just the tip of a vast organisation. The number of people working at airfields had more than doubled, not just because more aircraft were operating from the average airfield, but

An Avro Lancaster of No. 33 Squadron landing using a FIDO system at RAF Graveley, May 1945.

The personnel needed to support an Avro Lancaster in 1942. Front row: Flying Control Officer, Parachute Packer, Meteorological Officer, Crew. 2nd row: twelve flight mechanics of different specialisms. 3rd row: bomb trolley with driver and three Armourers. 4th row: seventeen further ground crew with different specialisms. Back row: fuel bowser and crew, mobile workshop and crew.

also because new and different jobs were constantly being created as each part of the organisation spawned new specialisms. New equipment on aircraft and within the fabric of the site required new specialists to maintain and operate it. Emergency services, for example, went from small numbers of fire engines and ambulances backed by a station sick bay, to an array of modern and specialist vehicles for not only fighting fires, but also quickly dismantling and removing wreckage to clear runways, and supported by substantial medical centres. Perversely, personal fire-fighting equipment seemed to take a backward step, as the bulky, fireproof asbestos suits introduced in 1937 were withdrawn in the middle of the war, as they were too large and unwieldy to allow the wearers to enter modern aircraft. Instead, firefighters had little more protection than their steel helmets and blue serge uniforms.

The growing complexity of aircraft, and the size of their crews, bomb and fuel capacity, and specialist equipment were driving factors in the growth of airfield sites. Bomb stores early in the war needed to contain enough munitions for about one week's use by the squadrons on the airfield, which might despatch a few dozen aircraft a week, each carrying 907–1,814kg (2,000–4,000lb) of bombs. By 1944, thirty or

forty aircraft a night could be despatched, each with anything up to 9,072kg (20,000lb) of bombs on board. Stores had to be bigger, containing hundreds of tons of bombs of different sizes and types. The infrastructure and personnel had to be on hand to move large numbers of bombs safely and rapidly in and out, while the increase in the number of bomb and fuse types led to more Armourers qualified in specialist areas. Fuel storage went through a similar expansion, as did oxygen stores.

A tractor pulls several trolleys of containers holding highly volatile incendiary bombs from a store.

Likewise the increase in technological aids on the aircraft for navigation and communications needed more specialists. These men and women needed designated workshops to carry out their trades, and storerooms to keep their spare parts and tools. They also, of course, needed accommodation, feeding, medical support, and a certain level of entertainment, all of which needed buildings and more staff to run them, who in turn needed their own accommodation, and so on. Thus the size and complexity of sites grew.

New organisations were needed to cope with the expanding numbers of support staff. Servicing Echelons had begun to be formed in Fighter Command in 1941, followed by the other Commands later in the war. These took the expanded number

An Avro Lancaster receiving attention from a range of different specialists during routine maintenance.

of ground crew needed to maintain the aircraft (specifically those needed for major inspections, repairs, and specialist maintenance) and formed them into their own unit, easing the administrative and disciplinary burden on squadron commanders. In Bomber Command, this side of the organisation was also eased in 1943 with the introduction of the Base system, whereby airfields were formed into groups of three. One station would be the Base Headquarters, with administrative control over two subsidiary

RAF Prestwick, in 1945, showing just some of the thousands of aircraft that arrived there from North America during the war. Very careful handling and control was needed to ensure safety.

satellite airfields, reducing the number of staff the latter needed. Further steps to help streamline and simplify the organisation of airfields, allowing staff to concentrate on doing their jobs to the best of their ability, included cutting out much of the 'spit and polish' that went with military life. For example, parade grounds were not included in the airfields built during the war. While military discipline and tidiness needed to be maintained, it was kept to a minimum wherever possible.

After the war, the number of airfields began to decline almost immediately, although it was not a speedy process. Depending on the terms under which the land was acquired, some sites were returned to their original owners, but many sites were placed onto a 'Care and Maintenance' basis. This meant that buildings and facilities were mothballed and only basic work carried out to keep them functional, while the land might be leased out to local farmers for grazing. Sometimes airfields on 'C&M' were leased to private businesses or industry, and many were not fully disposed of until well into the 1950s. As large open areas, with good infrastructure and solid buildings, drainage and other facilities, they had proven ideal locations for industrial or housing estates, and many have been further buried under concrete in subsequent years.

This post-war view of RAF Henlow shows the contrast between pre-war and wartime building styles, with the wartime sites being well spaced out to protect against bombing.

FURTHER READING

There is a vast array of books on airfields and airfield buildings available, ranging from essentially picture books of building types to in-depth station histories. Below are some of the books that the author judges to be most useful for finding out more.

'ACTION STATIONS' SERIES

Bowyer, M.J.F. *Action Stations 1: Wartime Military Airfields in East Anglia 1939–1945*. Patrick Stephens Ltd, 1979.

Halpenny, B.B. *Action Stations 2: Military Airfields of Lincolnshire and the East Midlands*. Patrick Stephens Ltd, 1981.

Smith, D.J. *Action Stations 3: Military Airfields of Wales and the North-West*. Patrick Stephens Ltd, 1981.

Halpenny, B.B. *Action Stations 4: Military Airfields of Yorkshire*. Patrick Stephens Ltd, 1982.

Ashworth, C. *Action Stations 5: Military Airfields of the South-West*. Patrick Stephens Ltd, 1982.

Bowyer, M.J.F. *Action Stations 6: Military Airfields of the Cotswolds and Central Midlands*. Patrick Stephens Ltd, 1983.

Smith, D.J. *Action Stations 7: Military Airfields of Scotland, the North-East and Northern Ireland*. Patrick Stephens Ltd, 1983.

Halpenny, B.B. *Action Stations 8: Military Airfields of Greater London*. Patrick Stephens Ltd, 1984.

Ashworth, C. *Action Stations 9: Military Airfields of the Central South and South-East*. Patrick Stephens Ltd, 1985.

Quarrie, B. *Action Stations 10: Supplement and Index*. Patrick Stephens Ltd, 1987.

An updated series of 'Action Stations: Revised' has more recently been issued by Crecy Publishing.

'MILITARY AIRFIELDS' SERIES

Delve, K. *The Military Airfields of Britain: Southern England.* Crowood Press, 2005.

Delve, K. *The Military Airfields of Britain: East Anglia.* Crowood Press, 2005.

Delve, K. *The Military Airfields of Britain: Northern England.* Crowood Press, 2006.

Delve, K. *The Military Airfields of Britain: South-Western England.* Crowood Press, 2006.

Delve, K. *The Military Airfields of Britain: Northern Home Counties.* Crowood Press, 2007.

Delve, K. *The Military Airfields of Britain: Wales and West Midlands.* Crowood Press, 2007.

Delve, K. *The Military Airfields of Britain: East Midlands.* Crowood Press, 2008.

OTHER TITLES

Falconer, J. *RAF Airfields of World War Two.* Midland Publishing 2012.

Francis, P. *From Airships to the Jet Age.* Patrick Stephens Ltd, 1996.

Innes, G.B. *Aviation Pocket Guide: British Airfield Buildings of the Second World War.* Midland Publishing, 1995.

Innes, G.B. *Aviation Pocket Guide: British Airfield Buildings Vol. 2: The Expansion and Inter-war Periods.* Midland Publishing, 2000.

Smith, D.J. *Britain's Military Airfields 1939–1945.* Patrick Stephens Ltd, 1989.

Many old airfields are marked in some way, such as this memorial at RAF Moreton-in-Marsh, Gloucestershire.

PLACES TO VISIT

There are hundreds of airfield relics scattered around the country, ranging from near-complete sites to solitary buildings or sections of runway. This section highlights a few of the more comprehensive sites, where you can find clusters of buildings in good condition. Most are also supported by aviation museums or other interpretation. For advice on how to find more complete lists of sites or particular building types, please see the end of this section.

Imperial War Museum Duxford, Duxford, Cambridgeshire CB22 4QR. Telephone: 0207 4165000. Website www.iwm.org.uk/visits/iwm-duxford – This is easily one of the most impressive aviation museums in the UK, as well as being a well-preserved and indeed still functioning airfield. Although some of the hangars and other buildings are post-war, or purpose-built for the museum, much of the flight line and the Technical Site behind it are original 1920s–1940s buildings. Apart from the hangars, squadron offices, and various workshops, there is also the Station Headquarters and Guard Room either side of the staff entrance on the A505. The Motor Transport Sheds are still intact and in use, while the rare gun butts are also in good repair. On the northern side of

BELOW LEFT
Many of Duxford's exhibition hangars are original, allowing aircraft to be seen in their original surroundings.

BELOW RIGHT
Large parts of the Technical Site at IWM Duxford are original, as is the Domestic Site across the A505.

the A505 is the Domestic Site, including messes and barrack blocks. Many of these former domestic buildings are used as museum offices or stores, and are not generally accessible to the public. However, on air show days (which are well worth a visit for their own sake) public parking is in this area and you can see the buildings up close.

Many buildings at IWM Duxford are still in use, like these Motor Transport Sheds.

Royal Air Force Museum at Hendon, Grahame Park Way, Hendon, London NW9 5LL. Telephone: 020 82052266. Website: www.rafmuseum.org.uk/london – Although much smaller than IWM Duxford, this is another site of national importance, and there are a number of interesting buildings. The Grahame White Factory and Watch Office (Hangar 2) date from the First World War, but next to them is a cluster of Expansion Period workshops (now the museum's own workshops and 'Claude's Café'), and a parachute packing shed (Building 69) with its distinctive raised centre section in the roof, to enable parachutes to be hung up for inspection. The Historic Hangars (Hangars 3 and 4) date from the First World War but were used right through the inter-war period and the Second World War, and while their ends have been removed and they are encased in an outer shell, you can look up to see the original Belfast roof trusses. The RAF Museum's other site at Cosford (Shifnal, Shropshire TF11 8UP, Telephone: 01902 376 200) also has wartime hangars.

Some of the Expansion Period buildings at Hendon. This area has been considerably renovated as part of their 'RAF100' centenary programme.

The Lincolnshire Aviation Heritage Centre, East Kirkby, Spilsby, Lincolnshire PE23 4DE. Telephone: 01790 763207. Website: www.lincsaviation.co.uk – This is an active airfield in Lincolnshire that is famous for its Avro Lancaster 'Just Jane', which at the time of writing is regularly taxied around the airfield, although there are plans in motion to bring her back to flying condition. 'Just Jane' is only one of the attractions on site. The original control tower has been restored, and there are various other airfield buildings containing an impressive museum collection.

The old Officers' Mess at RAF Middleton St George, with a statue of Canadian VC winner Pilot Officer Andy Mynarksi.

Kenley Airfield, Kenley, Surrey CR3 5LZ. Website: www. kenleyrevival.org – Kenley claims to be the most complete RAF fighter station still in existence. The site still operates as an airfield for gliders, and has runways and taxiways laid out on the original wartime plan. Numerous buildings and dispersal areas survive, as does a rifle range.

One of the surviving gun butts at IWM Duxford.

The site has numerous interpretation boards, and self-guided walks can be downloaded from their website.
Airworld Aviation Museum, Caernarfon Airport, Dinas Dinlle, Caernarfon LL54 5TP. Telephone: 01286 832154. Website: www.airworldmuseum.com – This is another museum that is at an active airfield. The former RAF

A surviving shed at the flying boat base at Llanfaes. Several slipways also survive.

Llandwrog, it is now Caernarfon Airport, and it includes a good example of a 1941 control tower that is still in use, while the nearby museum includes aircraft, an aviation collection, and an exhibition dedicated to the RAF Mountain Rescue Service. Just outside Beaumaris, on the other side of the Menai Straits, there are the remains of the flying boat base at Llanfaes. Some of the slipways and buildings still survive.

RAF Drem, Arts and Crafts Gallery, Fenton Barns, Drem, East Lothian EH39 5BW. Website: www.rafdrem.co.uk – RAF Drem also has a small museum, and there are a number of surviving buildings including two hangars in the surrounding Fenton Barns Retail Village.

This list only scratches the surface. For the more intrepid airfield spotter, buildings and infrastructure can be found all over the country. There are concentrations of them (without

The former control tower of RAF West Malling is all that survives on what is now a housing estate. Since this photograph was taken, it has opened as a coffee shop.

supporting museums) at Kemble (now Cotwolds Airport), Hullavington, Manby, West Raynham, Bicester, Church Fenton, North Weald, and Kirton-in-Lindsay, to name but a few. To find some in your area, or for particular building types, some excellent online resources are available.

The Airfield Research Group is a mine of information, including a forum accessible to non-members (www. airfieldresearchgroup.org.uk), and the Airfields of Britain Conservation Trust has a searchable list of over 2,000 sites (www.abct.org.uk). At www.ukairfields.org.uk, the owner has attempted to list all UK airfields, aviation memorials, and other associated sites. The site www.controltowers.co.uk is, as the name suggests, a list of control towers and their basic histories, and again can be searched by airfield name. A large number of old airfield buildings now enjoy listed status, and can be found on the Historic England database at www.historicengland.org.uk. Some areas also have their own, more specific websites, such as the Bomber County Aviation Resource (www.bcar.org.uk), which has a wealth of information on sites in Lincolnshire.

The memorial to No. 617 Squadron at their former base of RAF Woodhall Spa.

INDEX